D0561266

BONE SONGS

BONE SONGS

André Gregory

Developed in collaboration with
Liz Sherman and Scott Cohen

THEATRE COMMUNICATIONS GROUP
NEW YORK
2006

Bone Songs is copyright © 2006 by André Gregory,
Liz Sherman and Scott Cohen

Bone Songs is published by Theatre Communications Group, Inc.,
520 Eighth Avenue, 24th Floor, New York, NY 10018-4156.

All rights reserved. Except for brief passages quoted in newspaper, magazine, radio or television reviews, no part of this book may be reproduced in any form or by any means, electronic or mechanical, including photocopying or recording, or by an information storage and retrieval system, without permission in writing from the publisher.

Professionals and amateurs are hereby warned that this material, being fully protected under the Copyright Laws of the United States of America and all other countries of the Berne and Universal Copyright Conventions, is subject to a royalty. All rights including, but not limited to, professional, amateur, recording, motion picture, recitation, lecturing, public reading, radio and television broadcasting, and the rights of translation into foreign languages are expressly reserved. Particular emphasis is placed on the question of readings and all uses of this book by educational institutions, permission for which must be secured from the publisher.

The Shackleton excerpts are from *Endurance: Shackleton's Incredible Voyage*, by Alfred Lansing, Carroll & Graf Publishers, New York, 1959, 2002; the Rilke quote is from *Letters of Rainer Maria Rilke 1910–1926*, W. W. Norton & Company, New York, 1969; the T. S. Eliot quote is from "East Coker," *Four Quartets*, A Harvest Book, Harcourt, Inc., New York, 1943, 1971 renewed.

This publication is made possible in part with public funds from the New York State Council on the Arts, a State Agency.

TCG books are exclusively distributed to the book trade by Consortium Book Sales and Distribution, 1045 Westgate Dr., St. Paul, MN 55114.

LIBRARY OF CONGRESS CATALOGING-IN-PUBLICATION DATA
Gregory, André.
Bone songs / by André Gregory ; developed in collaboration
with Liz Sherman and Scott Cohen.—1st ed.
p. cm.
ISBN-13: 978-1-55936-284-9
ISBN-10: 1-55936-284-7
I. Sherman, Liz. II. Cohen, Scott. III. Title.
PS3607.R487B66 2006
811'.54—dc22
2006013098

Book design and composition by Lisa Govan
Cover design by Mark Melnick
Cover image (top) from Charles Lindsay's *Science Fiction* project;
www.charleslindsay.com

First Edition, November 2006

For Cindy

You rescued me from Antarctica.
You reached out your hand and never let go.
You changed my work.
You changed my life.

For Nicolas and Marina

With great love

Once the realization is accepted that even
between the closest human beings
infinite distances continue to exist,
a wonderful living side by side can grow up,
if they succeed in loving the distance between them
which makes it possible for each to see
the other whole against the sky.

—RILKE

Contents

Acknowledgments

Special thanks to Liz Sherman whose dogged and ferocious tenacity kept the project from disappearing into the mists of Antarctica.

Thanks also to Lyn Austin of Music-Theatre Group, Fred Berner, Sally Davis, Jack Doulin, Deborah Eisenberg, Barbara Feldman, John Ferraro, Fine Arts Work Center in Provincetown, Shawn-Marie Garrett, Julie Hagerty, Jackie Judd, Rocco Landesman, Margo Lion, Karen Lordi, Sidney Mackenzie, Mark Murphy and everyone at REDCAT, Bruce Odland, Cynthia O'Neal and Friends Indeed, The Laura Pels Foundation, Carol Rizzo, Leslie Silva, Olga Silverstein, Kathy Sova, Monina von Opel and The Vineyard Playhouse.

And a special thanks to Scott Cohen and Larry Pine.

BONE SONGS

Old men ought to be explorers.

—T. S. ELIOT

LOST LOVING

A very, very old man is keening and mourning the wife he lost many, many years ago. He's standing out on an ice floe in Antarctica. His beard is covered with ice. His goggles are covered with ice. He sings this song, a kind of mournful keening:

THE EXPLORER

Lost loving in the cradle touch, crystals in my hand, and
mirrors make your heart reflect the kiss I never knew.
If only clocks were toys, and time an exercise in being,
and all the world were set up right so daffodils were poetry
and stars were things you ate at night to grow up straight
and strong, wrong and right would not exist and I could
still be young again, and all the things I never did I'd never
do again.

    But now is not the time to weep, my eyes are dry with
knowing that distances are here to stay but I am not eternal,
and words like "love" and "seeing you" are things we learn in
school, but no one tells what happens next when you're far out
at sea, and compasses are frozen fast with chemistry technology,
so linear is circular and nothing's very real.

    I mean like you, I mean like me, I mean like all the others.
Wash away the days I did and wash away I didn't where loving
was confusion's mate and better late than never.

    So wide the wound and opening, so grave and great
the entering, that whales can dance to crooning gulls on
harps whose strings' harpooning makes a stone that bleeds,
a shell that talks and fog that whispers, walks and moans,

of moons it never sees again until the waves can stop
their dance.

Turn on the lights,
turn on the lights,
the days are done,
I want the nights.

QUINTET

A Musical Overture

*Antarctica. The Explorer is joined by the honeymooning Younger He
and Younger She and their older selves—Older He and Older She.
They come and go as they see fit throughout the play.*

THE EXPLORER

When you get to be my age . . .

YOUNGER HE

Oh,
years from now when you and I are old—

THE EXPLORER

And gray.
When you get to be my age, you wonder if this day will be your—

OLDER SHE

Last night I dreamt I was back in life again.
I dreamt I was your wife again. Imagine—

OLDER HE

Imagine.
The sound of a train at night.
A whistle in the dark.

THE EXPLORER

We whistle in the dark for just a little while.
And then you count the days on one—

YOUNGER SHE

Hand in hand.

YOUNGER HE

Together we look forward to the day—

THE EXPLORER

And to the night when now I lay me down.

OLDER SHE

So many moments.

OLDER HE

So many things we never said.

OLDER SHE

We tried.
But then I died.
You know.

OLDER HE

We tried.
But then you died.
I know.

OLDER SHE

For so many years the fears of growing old
and then you . . .

YOUNGER HE

Are you ready?

THE EXPLORER

Ready or not when you get to be my age.
When now you lay me.
I mean, when now I lay me—

OLDER SHE

Down on an antique pillowcase,
a box of lace.

OLDER HE

The weeping willow
that was a gift to one you loved.
The years are passing by.

OLDER SHE

I know.

YOUNGER HE

The fears are only fears.

YOUNGER SHE

I know.

THE EXPLORER

I know absolutely nothing.
That's the way it is
when you get to be my age.

YOUNGER SHE

I love the sound of church bells
early in the morning.

THE EXPLORER

A word of warning:
the ground grows hard and cold.

YOUNGER HE

I love to sleep—

YOUNGER SHE

With you.
Beside me.

YOUNGER HE

I love the way you hold me when you're—

THE EXPLORER

Inside me a younger man
who knows no time at all.
Yet now I lay me down—

YOUNGER HE

To sleep with you—

THE EXPLORER

To weep for you no more.

YOUNGER SHE

I love the sound of church bells
early in the morning.

THE EXPLORER

How I loved you.

YOUNGER HE

And I love you—

YOUNGER SHE

I truly do.

THE EXPLORER

Deep in the ground
and not a sound
when soon they lay me down to sleep.
At last
under an Arctic moon.

YOUNGER SHE

I love the sound of church bells
early in the morning.

THE EXPLORER

Deep in the ground
and not a sound
when soon they lay me down to sleep.
At last
under an Arctic moon.

ARCTIC
LOVE SONG I

Antarctica. A tiny icebreaker. The young couple on their honeymoon, on the ship's deck, sailing down to the bottom of the world.

YOUNGER HE

I saw a polar bear!

YOUNGER SHE

You didn't.

YOUNGER HE

I did.

YOUNGER SHE

Where?

YOUNGER HE

Over there. Just as the sun was setting.

YOUNGER SHE

Billions of stars. The blackest of nights.
I'm so glad we came.

YOUNGER HE

So am I.
I've never seen anything.
Quite so black.

YOUNGER SHE

And white.
It's wonderfully white in the daylight.

(The Explorer enters.)

THE EXPLORER

I hear you're on your honeymoon.
Strange place for a honeymoon.
I come down here every year,
as soon as the ice breaks in springtime.
I'm looking for my wife.
I'm looking for clues.
I look at the two of you and try to remember the two of us.
Way back then.
A honeyed moon.
Just imagine.
Down here at the South Pole.
The three of us, strangers, standing at a ship's railing—
you with a whole life ahead and me sailing backwards into time.
What a strange thing, a lifetime.
What will you do when you get home?

YOUNGER HE AND YOUNGER SHE

We'll be happy.

THE EXPLORER

Good luck! Take me with you.

YOUNGER HE

Look. A shooting star!

YOUNGER SHE

Where?

YOUNGER HE

There, and there, and there . . .

ALL THREE

Make a wish.

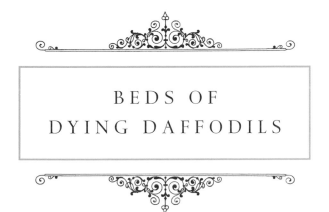

BEDS OF
DYING DAFFODILS

Antarctica.

THE EXPLORER

I need a rest from all the ghosts. White robes with strands of blood,
a past which doesn't let me breathe, the hating and the haunting.
I look for meanings in the cracks. I try to heal the fissures. The
vase that cracked so long ago is filled with pus and tears.

I try to smile, I try to keep on going. But this, my earth, is
scorched to bone, so delicate disintegrates and dust to parch the
lips to crack won't let me sing, won't let me kiss, and even eating
pains the gums so any action strains a brain like wells gone dry,
which howl out, "No!" to buckets dropped and dropped again.

So vain the search, so hard the quest, and I don't have the
energy to try again, to try in vain. To walk out bare, and let the
rain and frosty pellets punctuate futility of skin too thin.

And rotten is the apple now and so aghast the worm, that
every time I look at you and every time you look at me is such an
effort of the will that gray my hair and hardening of arteries that
also beg for Sunday's rest a Sabbath ease, a little moment of repose.

But, no, godamnit all to hell, the planet keeps on turning.
And burning eyes, their whos and whys, look out at you all
black and blue and beg for rest and beg to stop.

But it goes on, you can't get off so frantic shake the limbs
as if the earth did quake a reckoning so hard to take, I cannot
walk, I cannot talk, and yet I must or else the dust will blanket
me in beds of dying daffodils.

WHISPER TO ME

YOUNGER SHE

Whisper to me.
Whisper soft and low,
not the thousand ways you think you love me so,
but whisper to me low of little things.
I don't know,
the wings of woodland butterflies fluttering through a summer's
sky,
let's say,
a simple ordinary day.
Not the highs and lows of joy and sorrow,
simply what you did today
and what you'd like to do tomorrow.
For just this one night and perhaps another,
I need to be your sister and you my brother.
Just whisper to me,
whisper soft and low.

YOUNGER HE

But I want to touch your fingers with my fingertips,
singing you love songs of sweet delight
every moment of this star-drenched night.
My God,
I love you so.

YOUNGER SHE

No.
No.

Let go.
Only whisper to me,
whisper to me.
Tell me, if you must,
but without a sound how much
and if and when and why.

YOUNGER HE

But I want so to sigh and kiss your ifs away.
I love you so.

YOUNGER SHE

No.
No.
I know you do, but . . .

YOUNGER HE

Listen.
Just play with me a little while,
my darling sweetheart,
let me whisper you apart and yearn . . .

YOUNGER SHE

No.
No.
Learn to stay beside me, silent.
Open heart but not tonight
inside me drenched in honeyed mead.
Not tonight.
This must be our silent polar night.

YOUNGER HE

But I need you so.

YOUNGER SHE

I know you do.
I know.
Me, too.

But not out loud and not tonight.
Turn out that light and let's learn to whisper,
let's learn to be mute,
learning to dance to a ghostly flute,
let's start together
and apart.
Mostly I love you.
Mostly I do.
Don't ask for more.
I'll close the door
and if I do, my ears will close
like an autumn rose.
Whisper to me,
whisper to me,
songs of the heart
fiercely together
but softly and honestly apart.

YOUNGER HE

Oh all right.

EQUIVOCATE

OLDER SHE

I think my goose is cooked.

OLDER HE

They can make mistakes.
They're only human.

OLDER SHE

No they're not.
We haven't seen one doctor who is human.
Don't equivocate.
Don't always try and make everything all right.
This is not all right.
Nothing about this is going to turn out right.
What are we going to do?

(Pause.)

OLDER HE

I wonder what that really means.
Equivocate.
I wanted to ski and I never did.
I wanted to learn Hebrew and I never did.
You wanted to learn about the stars.
I wanted to go to the South Pole, God knows why.
Never did. Never will. Too late.
When I was young, I thought,
Each day I'm going to open the dictionary and learn a new word.

It'll be a discipline.
Didn't do it. Wish I had.
Equivocate.
I wonder what that means.

OLDER SHE

Hedge, pussyfoot,
weasel, waffle.

OLDER HE

How do you know that word?

OLDER SHE

Did you ever have an affair?

OLDER HE

Excuse me?

OLDER SHE

I asked if you ever had an affair.

OLDER HE

No.
Of course not.

(Pause.)

Yes.
I did.
Once.

OLDER SHE

Only once in all of those years?
I don't believe you.

OLDER HE

Only once.
Yes.

OLDER SHE

Why?

OLDER HE

Why did I do it or why only once?

OLDER SHE

Both.

OLDER HE

Do we have to?

OLDER SHE

Tell me why.
Why did you do it?
How could you?

OLDER HE

Please don't.

OLDER SHE

I hate you.

OLDER HE

You asked me.
You wanted to know.

OLDER SHE

I don't even know who you are.
After all of this time.
Goddamn you to hell.
Tell me why you did it.
Did it make you feel better?

OLDER HE

For a week or two.
Mostly I felt ashamed.
Ashamed and shitty and dead.

OLDER SHE

That's what I'll be soon.
Shitty and dead.

(Pause.)

OLDER HE

I'll always be with you.

OLDER SHE

No you won't.
And anyway it doesn't help.

THE EXPLORER

We were a golden couple, you and I.
Nick and Nora Charles.
The Thin Man.
Teeny martinis.

OLDER HE AND THE EXPLORER

Remember?

OLDER SHE

Not a care in the world.
Take care of yourself.
Promise?

OLDER HE

I do.

OLDER SHE

Take care of the kids.
Promise?

OLDER HE

I do.

OLDER SHE

Till death do us part.

OLDER HE

Till death do us part.

OLDER SHE

Good night, Gracie.

OLDER HE AND THE EXPLORER

Good night, George.

ARCTIC
LOVE SONG II

Listen to Me

Antarctica. To Younger He and Younger She:

THE EXPLORER

Listen to me. Those little things, you know, the ones you want
to say and can't, some tiny failure of nerve, they go into the body
and disappear, they do, tiny vipers waiting to take over. Unsaid
words harden, congeal, they do, and become a mountain of ice.
And there is no ice pick huge enough and no blowtorch hot
enough and no words sharp enough to break and burn the ice away.

Have you ever seen an iceberg up close? A huge one is
coming in on the starboard bow! I saw it through the captain's
telescope—brilliant white against the blackness of the night.
A mountain of ice. It's almost on top of us.

Listen.

(The older couple from far away:)

OLDER HE

That poem you loved so much, remember?

OLDER SHE

No.

OLDER HE

How did it go?

OLDER SHE

No.

OLDER HE

Yes. I'm sure you do. Come to the edge.

YOUNGER HE

Come to the edge.

YOUNGER SHE

I can't. It's too deep.

YOUNGER HE

Come to the edge.

YOUNGER SHE

It's too high.

YOUNGER HE

Come to the edge.

YOUNGER SHE

We might fall.

YOUNGER HE

Come to the edge.

BOTH COUPLES

And they came and he pushed them and they flew.

WAKING THE SPIDERS ON THE FLOOR

*Things You Should Have Said
but Never Could*

OLDER HE

(In his head:)

In me is the spirit of and silent night
and all the meditations
Tibetan bells Franciscan chants
the spirit of and silent night
and tenderness of privilege
to priestly smoke in reverence
to gain eternal life
and know that heaven's gates swing wide for me in God's embrace
and saccharine the sweetly grace divine
divine the spirit of and silent night
the wise men come to grovel at Saint Peter's throne
Saint Vitus's dance Hasidim grip
the ecstasy of chosen few elite
to light God's candle strong
belong the few
but not the throng
and I am one
and I am he
and yes I am the Buddha's knee
because I've searched
and still stayed pure
my suit is white with silk
and blue my eyes with chastity.
I am truly one of God's children.
I am his first born.

So don't touch,
handle with care,
hands off and this side up,
don't touch,
handle with care,
hands off and this side up,
because I am an artist,
an artist and therefore very delicate
and very valuable
and any harm that comes to me would be a loss so great
that high buildings would shake
with the echo of the grieving.
There is no way to underestimate,
no way,
no way at all.
I am an artist, deserving,
needy and most of all
I am very,
very greedy.

(A long silence.)

OLDER SHE

(In her head:)

Why don't you grow up and be a man?
Why don't you?
Why are you always so afraid?
Why do I have to be your mommy and your maid,
the center of your universe,
your sun and moon and stars and sky?
Why, why, oh why don't you grow up and be a man?

I know. I know.
You're the sweetest, nicest, kindest man I've ever met.
You're killing me with kindness,
thinking you're so fucking witty,

drowning me with your self-pity.
You're Mommy's darling little boy,
her Fauntleroy,
and I'll protect you.
I won't respect you but I'll protect you.
Oh yes, oh yes, thank you, thank you, thank you
for your help and tolerance and patience and loving understanding.
But Jesus Christ,
why don't you grow up and be a man?

(A long silence.)

OLDER HE

Don't forget your shawl. It's getting cold.

(In his head:)

I think you're afraid to take the gift I give. I do. Deep below the
surface of your grinning skin, even below the rage, deep down
around the bones you think you're filth, no good. You do. I've
heard you sobbing in the dark at night alone in another room.
It's not only because of me. It's lonely because of you. Under
your rage and energy and heat you're cold as ice and beat me up
in silence wanting, wanting something. Some undeciphered thing
from me, always from me, something that will make the whole
world right, something that will drive away the darkness of your
terrifying night. The dark of your disbelief in love. Your loathing
of a girl called "you." Your hatred of a man called "me."

I'm not the one to help you talk and walk and sing and
celebrate. I'm not. You must do it for yourself. Alone. Together.
I'm just a man. I'm not a prince, a shining knight, a god. I'm just
a man. At times I'm ordinary, undistinguished. Just imagine: mean,
manipulative and gross, stinking of mortality, imperfect, tense.

But I'm also kind and generous and blind to your vision
of yourself. I see you for what you also are—a thing of joy, alive,
intelligent and brave. And I'm perhaps the best you'll ever find,
not just because I'm kind, but because I'd never say to you,

"So let us finish what we start and if we can't then let us part."
I never would. I'm here for good. And bad. For better and for
worse. For better and for worse.

OLDER SHE

I hate bridge.

(In her head:)

I can, I can't. I will, I won't. I simply cannot listen for madness
whimpers at my door to wake the spiders on the floor and
everything you have to say I've heard you say, my dear, before.
I will not be a butterfly for you to pin and give a name, I will
not be a butterfly to giddy glide into the flame and burn for
your invention. I'm tired, too, and I can't sleep. And your
complaints don't help or ease the fear I have of razor blades, the
fear I have of Alpine heights, the fear I have of city lights . . .

I don't know who I am and that's the thing I fear the most.
And if you have to name the ghost, I mean if you insist, I'll blast
you to smithereens to bits with howl to pain and gruesome fits
and you and I can call it quits.

Your words are gates imprison me gesticulate articulate so
let us finish what we start and if we can't then let us part.

(Silence.)

I want my life.

(A long silence.)

OLDER HE

Where the hell did I put those keys?

WE'RE MONSTERS

In their heads:

OLDER SHE

We're monsters you and I.
Let's find fresh meat to eat and tear apart.

OLDER HE

Let's sink our fangs into another's heart.
Why not?

OLDER SHE

Why not?
You're bored with me. I'm bored with you.
I'm black and blue with loving you for all these years.
With all these tears for you for you always for you.

OLDER HE

I would love to smother someone new.
Kill her with kisses on her fresh pink lips.
Tear out her eyeballs with my fingertips.
Love her to death in a deathly life.
I'd be her vampire,
she'd be my wife.

BOTH

Chopping up children with a fork and knife.
I want to eat my way to hell.
I do.

OLDER SHE

I do.
With someone new.

OLDER HE

With someone new.

OLDER SHE

Not you.

OLDER HE

Not you.

(Silence.)

ARCTIC
LOVE SONG III

Shackleton's Diaries I

Antarctica. The icebreaker. To Younger He and Younger She:

THE EXPLORER

"Many of the icebergs appear like huge warehouses and grain elevators, but even more look like creations of some brilliant architect when suffering from delirium. Huge icebergs doomed to drift to and fro till the crack of doom splits and shivers them into a thousand million fragments. No animal life. No land. No nothing." —Shackleton's diaries. Nineteen hundred and fourteen. The year the Great War began.

ARCTIC
LOVE SONG IV

Ah, Youth!

YOUNGER HE

Oh, I see, we're just going to pretend . . .

YOUNGER SHE

Don't. Don't go there. Not tonight.

YOUNGER HE

When? Tomorrow? Next month? Next year? Our next incarnation?

YOUNGER SHE

I hate it when you use that tone of voice.

YOUNGER HE

What tone of voice? What tone of voice?

YOUNGER SHE

Forget it. You know what else I hate? I hate you. And the cold. And this boring, boring ship. And this insane honeymoon of yours.

YOUNGER HE

You wanted to come.

YOUNGER SHE

No I didn't.

YOUNGER HE

Yes, you did.

Younger She

Antarctica! For a honeymoon. For a honeymoon. A lot of ice floating around on a black sea. Good morning, lovely day to look at the ice. Hey, after lunch, why don't we . . . look at the ice? Icebergs by moonlight. How romantic!

Younger He

It's an adventure.

Younger She

Oh please, grow up. They don't marry people at sea, they bury them.

Younger He

I hate it when you use that tone of voice.

Younger She

And don't you ever call me cold again. Have you ever for just one moment thought that my kind of adventure might just be a teeny tiny bit different from yours? I mean, excuse me for being alive.

Younger He

Oh stop saying, "Excuse me for being alive."

Younger She

I'll say any goddamn thing I want to say. You know what I really hate about men?

Younger He

Don't do that. And I'm not men. I'm me.

Younger She

Well, that's another problem. I don't know who you are.

Younger He

Well maybe you should just try to find out. I have a friend—

YOUNGER SHE

Excuse me?

YOUNGER HE

I said I have a friend—

YOUNGER SHE

A what?

YOUNGER HE

A friend. A friend, for Christ's sake.

YOUNGER SHE

You never had a friend. You're a hermit. You never go out.

YOUNGER HE

That isn't true.

YOUNGER SHE

Yes, it is.

YOUNGER HE

No, it isn't.

YOUNGER SHE

I want to sleep alone tonight.

YOUNGER HE

You can't. There are only two cabins.

YOUNGER SHE

So, I'll sleep in the lifeboat.

YOUNGER HE

Oh, go to hell.

YOUNGER SHE

I don't have to. I'm there already.

(Silence.)

THE HEARTH
OF DARKNESS

OLDER SHE

Don't you dare use that tone of voice with me. Not now. Not now. This "thing" that I have . . .

OLDER HE

Can't we ever, ever, ever tell the truth?

OLDER SHE

Oh. I see. We're going to make my body a battleground for your truth. You self-righteous son of a bitch. This is not your body, it's mine.

OLDER HE

I want you to live.

OLDER SHE

You want me to what?! You haven't let me live my life. At least have the graciousness to let me live my death. *My* death. It's mine, not yours. And if I'm going to live . . . Oh my God, I wish I'd never met you.

OLDER HE

And I wish—

OLDER SHE

No, no more wishes, sailor boy. The wishing wells are poisoned. Leave me alone. For once in my life, leave me alone. I'm going to die and I haven't even begun to live my life.

The doctors didn't say that. They said you could live for years.
If only—

OLDER SHE

The doctors, the doctors. They don't really know a goddamn
thing. They don't. They're just men, more ignorant, fucking,
unfeeling men.

OLDER HE

You want to die, don't you?

OLDER SHE

Oh, I see, another neatly packaged theory of yours. That
precious, brilliant mind of yours we so admire.

OLDER HE

Don't you?

OLDER SHE

Wait a minute. Wait a minute, I get it. You *want* me to die, don't
you? It's your wishy-washy mealymouthed way of getting a
divorce. Let me do all the work. As usual. Nothing changes.
For once in your life, grow up.

OLDER HE

If I grow up, you'll be out of a job.

OLDER SHE

What the hell do you know? Mr. Smarty Pants. Mr. Theoretical.
Mr. Master Plan. You're a liar and a bastard and I hate you.

OLDER HE

Nothing changes. You always have.

OLDER SHE

What?

OLDER HE

You hate men. You hate yourself. You hate life. I've had it,
I can't take it anymore.

OLDER SHE

You can't take it anymore? It's my body those Nazi doctors are
pumping full of shit. The needle is in *my* arm. I'm a human
guinea pig. Not you. Me.

(Pause.)

Oh my God, what am I going to do?

OLDER HE

I know it's hard. I'll help.

OLDER SHE

You always do. That's what's killing me. Not cancer. You.

OLDER HE

You're an iceberg. A mountain of ice.

OLDER SHE

You must like the cold, sugar pie. You married me.

OLDER HE

My tastes could change.

OLDER SHE

And mine will, sailor boy, mine will. If I get through this alive.

OLDER HE

Oh, go to hell.

OLDER SHE

I don't have to. I'm there already.

(A very long silence.)

65

THROWING
THE BONES

The icebreaker goes into the most terrifying part of Antarctica, the bottom of the world, the Weddell Sea. This is the story they hear as they try to rock themselves to sleep:

THE EXPLORER

Want to hear a ghost story?

Every night, when the whole house was asleep, my mother, my father and I would meet to throw the bones.

We could have been three gunfighters in a western saloon waiting for the other to make his move.

We sat in a circle of electrical knowledge, cold, mean and silent. Power was the only thing that mattered as we sat on the floor late at night, surrounded by candles, sharing an ancient magic.

None of us, however, was very good at sharing. Each one wondered when the other would drop dead.

We threw the bones. We had the power of life and death over the innocents who slept upstairs. We infected their dreams. We threw the bones.

A strange kind of prayer, this chanting, the throwing of bones, the joining of hands. Not hands, claws, I thought. A joining of claws.

My mother's body was covered with scales, magnificent green magnets. How I envied her. I never dared to ask how long I would have to throw the bones and chant and weave before I too could be covered like her.

You didn't ask questions in that company. Conversation was at a minimum. Power was at a premium. Power was the only thing that mattered.

If looks could kill, if only looks could kill, I thought, as I watched my father. Year after year I waited. And waited. Watched for an opening.

I knew that she was waiting for me to kill him so that she could kill me.

I probably knew because I was always hoping that she would kill him so I could kill her. And then I would be the only one. Sitting alone, while the others slept, throwing the bones, and getting fat on power.

I would like to tell you what it feels like, this night madness, this midnight knowledge, this ice age crooning.

You don't ask for it. It asks for you. It demands your obedience.

I remember the first time, the time the cat came calling, entered my room, sat by my cradle, slept at my feet, split in two. This cat, as big as a panther to a small child, its fur the color of ice, split in two and became my father and mother. I never saw the cat again. But it lived in their eyes, smiling, suspicious and mean. "We had no choice," I hear my father's voice, "we had no choice."

And then my body seems to break in two, suddenly alive with death, my voice screams out of some pit, despairing and exulting, as I hurl myself against the walls, bruising my skin like a peach. I see patterns of electrical power dancing in the darkness. My ears speak. My mouth listens. The skin on my face begins to harden and my nose grows longer. Everything about me is tougher and sharper and different.

Once I was human. Not anymore. Never again.

I will sit forever now while others sleep, throwing the bones, laughing at the living, mutilated by my hunger, always waiting for my chance to murder the other two.

During the day, obediently, I would sit at the piano, playing the scales, watching my fingers. These hands were weak and flabby. But not at night. At night they played drums, scratched patterns in the woodwork, snuffed the life out of insects who wandered in by accident.

At night, these hands, bloated and heavy with power, would float up to my ears and press against my brain when the song began to come. There were flames in my throat as the song began to breathe. My teeth began to melt like icicles, and then harden like steel. And then there was no head or mouth or throat or teeth. Only the song. The beautiful song, caressing, crushing, bringing flowers to life out of nowhere.

The daylight hours were my sleepwalking time. I dragged my feet, trying to understand what was so great about school and friendship, birthday parties and children's games.

But night! Now that was something else. We may have hated each other, my mother, my father and I, hated each other to the point of murder, but we had a special language, a shared rhythm, a similar beat.

Gardens are choked by weeds the likes of us, you say. I'd be the first to admit it.

(Older He joins in.)

THE EXPLORER AND OLDER HE
So what! We had the time of our lives.

THE EXPLORER
By the time I was twelve I was nearly dead. Of exhaustion. Of dying by day and living at night. I had too many secrets. You don't approve?

THE EXPLORER AND OLDER HE
So what!

THE EXPLORER
You think this story is a perverse invention?

THE EXPLORER AND OLDER HE
So what!

THE EXPLORER
I'm not talking to you. I'm talking to my friends, the Bone People. They're all over town, you know. You might easily be

married to one and never know it. Pay attention to the way people move, to the voice, and especially to the eyes. Eyes that see too much and smell of fish. That's how you know the Bone People—those frantic exiles, chosen a million years ago, marked, tattooed loners who shriek at the moon and gather our grief in large bouquets. The Bone People are reflections in a frozen lake. They mirror our madness. Their song is an S.O.S.

THE MARCH OF TIME

Forties music begins to play softly in the background.

OLDER HE

"The March of Time," remember? Tommy Dorsey and Guy
Lombardo. Great stars at the Palace. Early in the morning of a
sweltering summer's night.

OLDER SHE

A way before air-conditioning.

OLDER HE

The great ocean liners safely anchored in port.

OLDER SHE

Milk trucks, remember, early in the morning, they'd bring in
bottles of fresh milk.

OLDER HE

Fresh milk and Wonder Bread. The world seemed completely
safe.

OLDER SHE

So it seemed. So it seemed.

OLDER HE

Fire escapes.

OLDER SHE

The 1940s.

OLDER HE

The 1930s.

OLDER SHE

And radio.

OLDER HE

The great Franklin Delano Roosevelt.

OLDER SHE

How we loved to sit around and listen to the radio. I'd walk a
mile for a Camel.

OLDER HE

On sweltering nights when it was just too hot, we'd sleep
together on the fire escape.

(A reverie:)

OLDER SHE

You know, my darling,
when I hear the babies waste, the nipples cry,
I wake up deadly straight and strong and you are still asleep,
and three A.M. means hours still till coffeecake and doing.

I see your naked lips and shriek the silence still
when sleeping pills no longer on the sill and night despair
awake with birds
whose beaks your lips resemble.

I long to sing a song we've never heard before,
to take the chance of losing you
to take the chance of losing me
to take the chance of winning us.

To tell the children soon to be born
that summer is the time of corn
but autumn is the time of love
when stars above and stars below
can whisper names like "you" and "me"
but you can't help and no one should
and here I lie alone
where touching you means touching me,
a ginger boy, a ginger girl,
who toss and turn and whistle burn
upon a glassy sea.

Two wounds reflect the icy heart that brought us close together,
and now we need incisive tools for after birth that clings like glue,
that clings to you that clings to me,
and begs to leave the garden
so one awake and one asleep is not our way of loving.

We talk and talk but still I see
that I can't sleep when you're away
and you can't dream when I'm not there . . .

(Younger He awakens sharply. In the dark:)

YOUNGER HE

How's that?

(Younger She, also awakening from sleep. In the dark:)

YOUNGER SHE

You were having a dream. Go back to sleep.

YOUNGER HE

See you in the morning.

(He nods off.)

YOUNGER SHE

It almost is.

YOUNGER HE

What?

YOUNGER SHE

Morning.

SEX IS
A LITTLE DEATH

OLDER SHE

Turn on the light. Wake up.

OLDER HE

Honey, it's the middle of the night.

YOUNGER SHE

Turn on the light.

YOUNGER HE

It's so late.

OLDER SHE AND YOUNGER SHE

That's the point. Turn on the light. Wake up.

OLDER HE AND YOUNGER HE

Do you know what time it is?

OLDER SHE AND YOUNGER SHE

It's time to cook up a storm.

OLDER SHE

Come on, sailor, come to me.

OLDER HE

Splash balloons my playful part,
extricate my ovulate.

OLDER SHE

Wait wait I can't,
come gin my tummy and bang my drum.

OLDER HE

Rock and roll with a rin tin tin.

OLDER SHE

Sever my lever with a lather of foam.

OLDER HE

Roam with a river and a rider with a whip.

OLDER SHE

Diver with a flipper and a flapper takes a sip.

OLDER HE

Sugar-coated crown to croon
pomegranate seed
to feed my hunger linger longer
suck the pluck
I have to pick my way
through forests uninhabited by birds of prey
but bees and wax to tax the curvature of spine
and whine and moan and reach
and fetch hot cauldrons bubbling honeydew
and melons burst their seams and spew forth pits
explode the buttons
and the rounded rump of stallions
breathing faster than
and than and than and than and than.

OLDER SHE

Wait, wait
I can't,
come topple my frenzy
with a squirrel and his nuts.

Older He

Ever so slowly on your tippy toes climb
and with nutmeg courage through primordial slime
take away take away take away
all the things like rings and watches and buckles on shoes
and I'll sing you the blues like you've never heard before
in arms blown up and puckered
for a lather and a croon.

Older She

Riding, riding wave upon wave
splash balloon my playful part
till the day and the dew and the dripping
of the last few moanings in the mornings
to come take away all the layers
that lie between the sheets of loving you till exhausted
and grieve it can't go on forever
breathing faster than
and than and than and than and than
balloons.

(Joined by Younger He, Younger She and the Explorer:)

All

Balloons.
I love balloons.
I love balloons
and I love you
and oh I love and oh and oh the letter O
is better than the letter O
is better than the letter
is better is better is bet bat bit bat bet bat bit bat bet bat bit bat
bet bat bit bat
boom.

Older She

The room's turning.

OLDER HE

Yes, darling, the room is turning.

YOUNGER SHE

It really is turning.

YOUNGER HE

Really.

(A long pause.)

OLDER SHE

Turn on the lights,
turn on the lights,
the days are done,
I want the nights.

The kids have left at first bereft,
but now I'm turning with a better burning,
the yearning for a second living,
not the mother's milky giving but something even wilder,
brighter.

Turn on the lights,
turn on the lights,
the days are done,
I want the nights.

For twenty years the wife and forks,
the nappies and the birth of storks.
I want to learn the burning of the turning of the stars,
the danger of the alleyways,
the nights and days that know no sleep.
I want to totter like the drunken tramp,
to watch the lighting of the lamp,
to sing and dance and rant and rave
and ride at dawn the tidal wave.

Turn on the lights,
turn on the lights,
the days are done,
I want the nights.

For twenty years the wife and spoon
but now the firefly, the flute, the loon.
I tell you this,
I tell you this,
the tiny kiss that you have known,
the tidy lips,
the tiny touch of fingertips.
Explode.

For twenty years I understood,
for twenty years I was the wood,
but now I hear another voice
and now I hear another choice.
The beating of my second heart sings you this song,
it's short, not long.
I lived the wife, the fork and knife,
But now I hear another life.

I'm not cute and I'm not pretty.
I'm a woman,
dangerous and witty the way the wind is dangerous
and the seasons and the floods and loving.
I'm dangerous the way change is.
I'm unexplored and undiscovered.

ALL

Turn on the lights,
turn on the lights,
the days are done,
I want the nights.

(Pause. Older He in the dark:)

OLDER HE

How's that?

OLDER SHE

You were having a dream. Go back to sleep.

OLDER HE

See you in the morning.

(He nods off.)

OLDER SHE

It almost is.

OLDER HE

What?

OLDER SHE

Morning.

IOWA

THE EXPLORER

She was falling asleep. I said, "Wake up, sweetheart, don't go to sleep. Sweetheart," I said, "there's something I have to say to you, we have to stay awake," I said.

OLDER HE

It broke my heart.

THE EXPLORER

Open.
You have to stay open, young man.
Don't go to sleep.

OLDER SHE

I'm so tired.

OLDER HE

What time is it?

OLDER SHE

I don't know.

(Silence.)

I have to sleep.
I do.

OLDER HE

Wait. Too fast.
Not yet.
Please.
Wait wait.
And remember.
Remember how we drove through the fields of Brittany.
On an autumn afternoon.
And we said, "My God, how in the world did the air get so clear?"

OLDER SHE

It was an autumn afternoon.
And the moon rose.

OLDER HE

We ran on the beach.

OLDER SHE

Jeepers!

OLDER HE

Barking at the moon.

OLDER SHE

Jeepers.
Creepers.
Dark to croon.

OLDER HE

Jeepers creepers where'd you get those peepers . . .
oh those weepers.

THE EXPLORER

Are you ready?

OLDER HE

I'll tell you more.

OLDER SHE

Do.
Tell me more.
My little boy. My man. My love.
Do. Do.

OLDER HE

Do you take . . .
Remember?
Remember that little church.
I wore white tie and tails and you were bathed in lace.
Shining.
Your face.

OLDER SHE

Shining.

OLDER HE

So white.

OLDER SHE

So black.

OLDER HE

Yes, yes,
your mother wore black.
Remember?
Why?
Look at that star.

OLDER SHE

Where?

OLDER HE

There.
And there.
And there.

Everywhere.
Shining.

OLDER SHE

Already dark.
Dead.
A billion years ago.

THE EXPLORER

It's time.

OLDER HE

I bet you don't remember the time I chased tiny Billy up a tree.

OLDER SHE

And splitting with laughter he peed on your head.
Dead. A billion years ago.
It all goes so fast.
A speck of dust upon a glassy sea.

OLDER HE

Remember.
The you.
The me.

OLDER SHE

It all goes so fast.

OLDER HE

Remember
my love for rhyme.
And your love for reason.
Every season celebrate.
It's not too late.

OLDER SHE

And then it is.
I have to sleep.

OLDER HE

Sweetheart,
remember.
Remember the embers of our burning time,
turning the rhyme of our together time.

YOUNGER HE

To have and to hold.

OLDER HE

Remember?

YOUNGER SHE

To have and to hold.

OLDER SHE

For a while.
And then grown,
gone.

OLDER HE

Too soon. Look at the moon.

THE EXPLORER

It's time.

OLDER SHE

To sleep.

OLDER HE

No. Not yet. Please. Just stay a little while.

YOUNGER SHE

For richer, for poorer.

OLDER SHE

A thousand and one nights,
My teller of tall tales.

So many words.
I'll stay for one more story and then I have to sleep.

OLDER HE

Once upon a time, when the earth was very small,
when winter's growth invisible . . .
I can't do it anymore.
I just don't have the words.
I'm so sorry.

OLDER SHE

Don't be sorry.
There's nothing to be sorry for.
I'll sing to you.

OLDER HE

My God.
I love you so.

YOUNGER HE

In sickness and in health.

YOUNGER SHE

In sickness and in health.

OLDER SHE

I'll sing to you.
It's the courageous step that makes
the blood a dam to burst on lawns of brown to green again.

YOUNGER SHE

(Takes over; her wedding vows:)

(Brown to green again) where you and I can learn to know
that differences are sacred.
When winter's growth invisible

becomes the softness of a spring
where brooks with blossoms overflow the banks of frozen ice . . .
And we can stop the brooding time
and we can just be nice.

YOUNGER HE

And all alone with fingers barely touching
but knowing that the touch can teach
the blind to see, the lame to leap.
Our eyes will be like apple trees,
our lips will burst with sap.

(Whispers to Younger She:)

What comes next? . . .
Oh yes:
confusion then our fusion makes and distances respected.
And I'll love you and you'll love me
but love will be an action.

YOUNGER SHE

And the time of tears will be the rain
that makes new flowers grow.
Such colors we have never seen,
perfumes that make us faint.
And watching us, a little child
whose wisdom's paint can etch this time,
so years from now when new confusions grow
like vipers by the lake,
the two of us can smile and say we've known this time before.

OLDER SHE

(To Older He:)

And lightning
will not be
the thing that cracks the tree in two,

but startlingly illuminates
the road that lies before us.

What comes next?

YOUNGER SHE

What comes next?

THE EXPLORER

Till death do us part.

YOUNGER SHE AND YOUNGER HE

Till death do us part.

OLDER SHE

I'm falling.
Asleep.
I'm falling for you.

OLDER HE

And I for you.

OLDER SHE

Good night, Cyrano.

ONE MORE TURN AROUND THE GARDEN

Lamb Stew

OLDER SHE

I died.

THE EXPLORER

Not to me.

OLDER SHE

I died.

THE EXPLORER

For me you'll always be . . .

OLDER SHE

Sweetheart!

(Older She begins dancing with the Explorer.)

I died.
You can imagine me for just a little while longer
but then I really have to go.

THE EXPLORER

Nothing's changed.

OLDER SHE

No.
Well . . . actually,
I have.

I'm younger.
And stronger.
And I live by myself now.

                    THE EXPLORER

Really?
So do I.

                    OLDER SHE

How do you like it?

                    THE EXPLORER

It's all right.
It's different.
I miss having someone I love in my bed.

                    OLDER SHE

Don't look at me, sailor boy.
Get yourself another dame.

                    THE EXPLORER

I'm trying.

                    OLDER SHE

No, you're not.
Not hard enough.

                    THE EXPLORER

Well, you're a hard act to follow.
I keep thinking of you.

                    OLDER SHE

Smile at what's passed
And live what is.

                    THE EXPLORER

Easier said than done.

(Pause.)

What's it like?
Where you are, I mean?

                    OLDER SHE

You'll find out.
Soon enough.

                    THE EXPLORER

God forbid.
Speaking of the divine,
I was trying to remember the recipe
for that amazing lamb stew of yours?

                    OLDER SHE

I don't remember.
Get yourself a cookbook.

                    THE EXPLORER

I have a cookbook.
I don't know how to use it.

                    OLDER SHE

Then get yourself another dame.

                    THE EXPLORER

You're impossible.

                    OLDER SHE

I always was.

(Pause.)

And the kids.
How are the kids?

THE EXPLORER

They're fine.

OLDER SHE

You promise?

THE EXPLORER

Would I lie to you?

(Pause.)

No,
really,
they're fine.

OLDER SHE

I'm so glad.
Thank you.
My God,
will you look at the time.
I really have to go.

THE EXPLORER

One last turn around the garden?

OLDER SHE

I'd love to.

(They stroll. She disappears. The Explorer returns with the younger couple, arm and arm.)

THE EXPLORER

It's time.
A time to rake the golden leaves of autumn
and a time to sit by running brooks in summertime,
fishing with a golden fly
and wishing that these endless evenings never die or fade.

"I have made my bed and lie in it forever,"
whispers the bride who's his no longer,
but the bride of God.
"I am on the other side," she says,
"now in the after wife,
laughter in the after life."
Apples on the apple trees for just a little while
while autumn ticking clocks and chimes of wishing wells
tell us nothing but the changing times.
Round and round again
from the rotting corpse in the frozen ground
to the baby bursting with a newly breath,
laughing away the chilling death,
willing to try again and again.
Time, time,
we will never understand
no matter what we rhyme or reason with a backward flip,
sipping the future season,
tasting the past.
"And will it last,
and will it last,"
you wonder as you wander back and forth
between the memories and imaginings.
Rings of wonder on a frozen face,
a box of lace,
a fox running for its life,
a woman who was his wife but now is only memories.
Don't understand,
don't even try.
We die and live again.
Perhaps.
Live.
Now in this very moment,
give the very best you can,
because before you know it,
yet again the frozen ground.
Round and round again,

the ticking clock,
a solitary rock beside the ocean tide,
a billion stars and silence.

Live.
Right now.
Between the silence and the ticking of a breath.
For soon is silence.
Live.
With laughter.
Now.
Before the after.
Life.

ARCTIC
LOVE SONG V

Shackleton's Final Diary Entry

Antarctica. Arvo Pärt piano music, "Spiegel im Spiegel," is heard.

THE EXPLORER

In the Antarctic Circle, summer has begun. It is now light twenty-four hours a day.

OLDER HE

The sun disappears only briefly near midnight leaving
a prolonged, magnificent twilight.

OLDER SHE

Ice showers lend a fairy tale atmosphere to the scene.

ALL

Millions of delicate crystals, thin and needle-like, descend in
sparkling beauty through the twilight air.

THE END

FRAGMENTS

erformed by myself (I can't imagine anyone else performing it because of the "autobiographical" fragments), *After Dinner with André* (what this text is sometimes titled in performance) becomes an extremely odd performance piece, a collage made up of the play *Bone Songs*, and fragments from my life, childhood and first marriage, as well as thoughts about love, death, time, and just about anything else that pops into my head in the moment faced with each night's particular audience. I am not quite sure from moment to moment what I am going to say next. That's what makes it somewhat dangerous. And then, of course, there's the pain of the remembrance of things past.

In earlier versions of *Bone Songs*, there were many more scenes on the icebreaker traveling to Antarctica. And since the Ancient (the Explorer) only appears on the boat, his role was much larger. This earlier version seemed more like a book for a Broadway musical: the Ancient was a lonely, garrulous widower, mostly self-involved, often insufferable—the young couple, his captive audience. In the current version, we are not sure whether we are listening to the Ancient or to André, the storyteller-raconteur—the audience becomes the young couple and, hopefully, it is the audience who is held captive.

This nonlinear device questions the nature of Time, a central concern in the play itself. It serves as a palate cleanser to the play, a kind of Brechtian distancing device that allows the audience the space in which to question, the space in which to be active. Which stories are real? Is André *André* or is André a character? Is the Ancient *André* or is he a character? What are we *really* seeing when we see an actor performing as himself within a role? What is Mask? What is Persona? These are questions that have always fascinated me, both in the theater and in my life. Who am I? An essentially spiritual question. I suppose in performances I become at times a kind of sophisticated upper-class Peer Gynt; at other times, an eccentric Prospero. I go on a journey through loneliness and grief to acceptance, celebration and thanksgiving. I really go there. Or do I?

As I wrote down the notes for this Fragments section (those thoughts that I share with the audience during the performance of *Bone Songs*), I thought of the last lines of Pirandello's *Six Characters in Search of an Author*, you know: "Illusion! Reality! Illusion! Reality! It's driving me crazy!" I also thought of Artaud: "The actor should be like a martyr signaling to us through the flames." It's hard to do that and not get burned.

In other words, given the questions about illusion and reality, given Peer Gynt, Prospero and Pirandello, given Artaud, the performance is also about the nature of theater itself.

I never particularly liked jazz, but whenever I was working on *Bone Songs*, I would play jazz on the stereo. Since it's taken me more than two decades to finish the play, I've heard a lot of jazz by now, and I love it.

I don't think I have ever *not* enjoyed one single moment of the directing process and, generally, it takes me at least a year and a half to rehearse a play. So I'd better enjoy it. I have always found acting quite pleasurable. Until I began writing myself, I had little sympathy for my writer friends who always seemed to be complaining about the pain of writing and the horrors of the writing process. Until I tried it myself. One night, at the time when I was again trying to finish the play, I was joining two friends for dinner at a small Italian restaurant. As I was about to go into the restaurant, I noticed it did not have a bar. I don't drink. But suddenly panicked by the realization that there was no bar, I went quickly to a bar across the street, and when I had finished my second martini, I thought, Oh my God, I am becoming a writer.

*T*hese autobiographical Fragments are incorporated during the live performance of Bone Songs. These thoughts spring from specific moments
in the play and so are noted here by their section title, where they might nat-
urally come up in performance. But what I'm inspired to talk about each
night changes every time.

Lost Loving

This play that I call *Bone Songs* is a kind of kaleidoscope or
carousel of songs, scenes, soliloquies and stories influenced by
Solomon's Song of Songs. In fact, I kept the quote from Song of
Songs: "Love is as strong as Death" on my desk as I wrote the play.

There's a theory amongst biblical scholars that the Song of
Songs may have been sung originally at weddings as a kind of fer-
tility rite, and once I thought of performing *Bone Songs* only at
weddings as a kind of celebratory, cautionary tale. Are there any
of you out there who are single and would love to get married?
(Show of hands) Well, join me, your pied piper, come work with
me on the play. Eight people who have worked on the play over
the years *have* fallen in love and gotten married. While the play
never seems to get done in New York, it does seem to have some
strange magnetic love force to it. A series of love songs. Are there
any New Yorkers here? You know the Algonquin. You go to the
Algonquin, and there's a chanteuse who's singing love songs and
some of them are bitter and some of them are gentle and some of
them are frightening and some of them are sweet. There are even
love songs about death. For instance, *Dancing in the Dark*. So, this
is a series of love songs.

This play was initially inspired by my wife, Chiquita, who died
fourteen years ago of breast cancer. Or, it was influenced by her in
a way. She was fifty-three when she died. And I wanted to give her
the words she might have said had she lived longer; and me the abil-
ity to answer those words. It was inspired by her, but now it's about
the mystery of time and the importance of talking, of being straight,
of being direct with the ones we love. I've actually been working
on this play for twenty-two years. And it's still not finished.

This is one of only a few times that we've ever done *Bone Songs* in a theater. I'm almost allergic to theaters. As a director, I've directed in ruined buildings, ruined theaters, ruined men's clubs, ruined riding stables. Why always ruins? I'm not sure. When we were doing *Vanya* for an audience of twenty-five or so, in the former ruins of the old Victory Theatre—it was a time before they closed the porno houses, kicked out the hookers and turned 42nd Street into a disinfected Disneyland—a fine old German film director walked into the theater (a tiny audience and the actors were all on the stage together), and he raved on and on and on to me about how much he loved the space: "Vot a vonderful space," he said in his accented English, "I love this space. I have never seen anything like it. Vonderful, vonderful." I asked him specifically what he found so wonderful. He thought for a moment. "How perfect. This ruin of a theater, on this ruin of a street, in this ruin of a culture, in this ruin of a nation, and here inside the ruin on a stage, this peculiar little group of actors who still care about culture and art, who still care about *Vanya*—just imagine—and watching them, this peculiar tiny little audience who also cares, and behind them in the vast empty auditorium, the ghosts of hundreds of thousands of audience members who in the past did something like this every night."

So this is kind of exciting, being here with you tonight. In this lovely theater instead of a ruin. I'm sort of getting over my allergy. I read the play by myself to a group of two thousand family therapists in Washington, D.C., which seemed kind of appropriate because I've probably been in more therapy than Woody Allen. (You'll see why later.) And I also read it for men who were HIV-positive. But this is one of the few times we've done it in a theater and with actors other than myself. This is my very dear friend Leslie Silva. And my very dear friend Larry Pine. Leslie has been rehearsing with me in *The Master Builder* for seven years. (We're nearly finished.) And Larry has been doing the same thing in *The Master Builder*. We hope to make that into a film soon. Larry and I have been working together for over forty years. *("Wow" from the audience)* Yes, "Wow" is right.

Previously, I called this evening *After Dinner with André*, partly because I like the title—it just seems sort of fun—and partly because if you saw the film *My Dinner with André*, you might remember that there are really four main characters. There's Wally and his girlfriend, Debbie. And there's André and his wife, Chiquita. Since Chiquita has died, this is *After Dinner with André*.

·→≡◎ ◎≡←·

I first started working on this play, as I said, twenty-two years ago, and back then it was only poetry. And this verse was an attempt to try to say things to my wife that we couldn't really speak about. It must have worked, because at the opening night party of the version I did with Twyla Tharp in 1983, my wife fainted. Since almost everybody here in the audience is younger than I am, you probably don't know that the concept of "relationship" didn't exist until the very late sixties. We didn't know what that meant. We didn't know that you could talk to each other or that you *should* talk to each other. So the original version was in verse. When my wife passed away, I started to invent a boat, an icebreaker and conventional scenes. And then this revised version, which partly takes place on the boat, I started to write after she passed away.

"Lost Loving" is the Explorer looking back, reminiscing, remembering when he and his wife were very, very young.

It's actually a little odd, that I wrote this at all. In verse, I mean. Because if it hadn't been for a very peculiar and unpleasant thing that happened to me when I was twelve years old, I might actually have become a writer instead of a theater director. Do you want to hear the story? Well, I was twelve years old and I was going to this very repressive, very Waspy English school. It was quite Dickensian. You know, we took Latin for six years. We learned Greek. The headmaster was actually a man named Mr. Strange, believe it or not. He had very long fingernails and he would clean them with a lead pencil.

And I was madly in love, well, as madly in love as a twelve year old could be, with a young girl, who I think might have been from the Kennedy family. And I would write her love poems. And these poems were completely innocent and nonsexual because, in fact, I didn't learn the facts of life till two years later from my roommate at boarding school, Herby Klipstein, from Fort Lauderdale, who told me the ugly details of how my parents brought me into the world.

So, these were really, really innocent love poems.

And we went out to California for the summer. And lived in this amazing house, which actually had belonged to this silent movie star. There was this long, circular driveway that was covered with plastic, which was new in those days, and it had these little lights underneath it. At night, when you drove up the driveway, it was sort of like driving across the moon, a stairway to heaven. And I would write her these love poems, you know, from California. And she would write me letters back. And then one day the letters stopped and I didn't hear from her. I was heartbroken for about a week or so. The way any teenager would be.

In the fall we went back to New York. One day I was walking with a couple of friends down the street, and she was up on the balcony of a building, on the first floor. (I didn't know that her family had moved.) And she invited us up. And we had Cokes and played Frank Sinatra or somebody. And suddenly her father came home. He grabbed me by the hair and very violently threw me down the fire escape. It's true. I think it was a mixture of oedipal shit and anti-Semitism. (There were only three Jews in school: there was my brother, me and a boy whose father had funded Mussolini, which didn't seem totally kosher.) And her parents were the heads of the parents' committee.

So I was brought in to see the headmaster and I was grilled for hours, being forced to admit what it was I had done to her. And, of course, because I didn't know anything about sex, I didn't know what they were insinuating. And so, at lunchtime—did any of you see *Gunga Din*? You remember when his sword is broken and his epaulets are pulled off?—they put me in front of the whole school. I was one of the honor students, and they stripped me of all my honors. I had planned to go to a school called Exeter, which was a very good school, and they wrote to say that I was morally unfit. If I went to a dance, somebody would immediately cut in. And at prize day in the spring, if I'd won a prize, say the Glen Essay Prize for Hero of a Lost Cause, they would say, "This year it's not being given."

The only thing that they couldn't take away from me was the school play because I was playing Petruchio in *The Taming of the Shrew*. It was going to be in three weeks and no little boy could possibly learn that role in anything less than six months. So, I came onstage, and I was a very shy, withdrawn, polite little boy, and I looked out at those Wasp motherfuckers and I was suddenly filled with rage—I knew how to act! It was probably one of the most terrifying Petruchios ever. As Beckett says, "Nothing is funnier than unhappiness." So, instead of becoming a writer or a poet, I became a theater director.

Well, the road to becoming a theater director was not that untroubled either. In my early twenties, my dream was to go to the Yale School of Drama. At Yale, I was interviewed by this legendary dean. I forget his name. After the interview, he said to me, "It's very hard to tell much about a young person in an interview. A young face is so blank, so empty, a tabula rasa. But every once in a while, I do meet someone who so clearly has absolutely no talent whatsoever that I have to beg them not to do it. Do something else. The theater is hard enough if you *have* talent. Become a lawyer, become a doctor, don't go into the theater." I was devastated.

I did get into a Martha Graham class for actors later on. I was mortified with embarrassment. I was quite overweight, very awkward and felt absurd in my leotards. But I gave myself to it with the same energy I gave to the Marines—I will try anything once as long as it doesn't hurt anyone. One day Graham comes over to me and whispers in my ear, "You know, darling, you have no talent . . . But you have such a big heart, one day you will become a great artist." Isn't that an amazing thing to say to a young person? Grotowski said there's no such thing as talent, only lack of talent.

Well, anyway, back in New York, after trying to get into Yale Drama, I heard you could get into Sandy Meisner's Neighborhood Playhouse without an interview. All you needed was a check. So I was instantly accepted but made the mistake of going in to talk to Mr. Meisner about life—art questions that were worrying me. A week before school began he took one look at me and decided

I was some sort of Harvard graduate, off-the-wall, rich kid flake—
he after all had been a Marxist in the Group Theatre—and by the
time I had gotten home, the school had called to say they made a
terrible mistake and didn't have a place for me anymore. My parents, who wanted me to become a lawyer, were thrilled. So the
first day of school I just showed up. Mr. Meisner says, "Didn't you
hear you're not in the school anymore?" "I did hear that, yes, sir,"
I say politely. I was a very reserved, shy, young man. "Well, go
home, you can't stay where you're not wanted," he said. Day after
day I showed up, and day after day, Meisner says the same thing.
After four months of this, Meisner may have been impressed by
my tenacity because he says, "Oh all right, all right, do you want
to do an independent activity?" An independent activity was this
exercise where you do something very simple like put on your tie
or shave while you say a little text. I was thrilled. This was the
moment I had been waiting for. The next day in class I draw a large
circle on the floor in chalk and I open a cardboard box and start
taking little live turtles out of the box. "What the fuck are you
doing? What kind of cockamamy independent activity is that?"
"It's a turtle race, sir." "Sit down, sit down," he said. So that was
the end of Neighborhood Playhouse.

Not knowing what to do next, I joined the Marines because
America had given my family sanctuary. It's hard to believe there
was a time of such innocence that I still believed in this country.
When I got out of the Marines—that's a whole other story—
I got into Lee Strasberg's acting class. Again, no interview, only a
check. My first scene—I was so excited—was a scene from *La
Ronde*. I was the young rich kid who has the hots for the maid.
My scene was with a young Israeli woman who eventually
became one of the greatest actresses in Israel. Her legs were blown
off in the Munich Olympic massacres. With prosthetics, she
learned to walk again and to go on with her acting career, and
years later I danced with her in Jerusalem. Anyway, I built up such
a sense of frustration because the maid would not go to bed with
me that I threw myself on the floor and began to eat the carpet.
"What the hell are you doing?" Strasberg asks. "What do you
mean?" I ask. "You are eating carpet," he says. "Yes, sir," I say.

"People don't do that," he says. "But I'm people and I just did it," I replied. "SIT DOWN," he says.

So that was the end of my acting career until twenty years later when I played the longest role in the history of film. I had told myself that if I weren't successful by the age of thirty, I would become a lawyer or a rabbi. At twenty-nine, out of desperation, I directed a new antiwar play, *P.S. 193* by David Rayfiel, which had the misfortune of opening the same night as the Cuban Missile Crisis. The critics hated it, the audience hated it, but I have been directing ever since.

If I talk too much, just shut me up. Someone once said to me that if I ever wrote a memoir I should call it *Sit Down and Shut Up*. Speaking of which, did any of you see that *New Yorker* cartoon where the André character and the Wally character are sitting at the table? The André character has a pie in his face yet is still talking, and the Wally character is screaming, "Shut up, shut up."

Quintet: A Musical Overture

On its simplest level, *Bone Songs* is verse, and of course you don't have to "understand" verse with your intellect. And it's music, which we also don't have to "understand." Perhaps all five characters are in some peculiar time zone, which is the past, present and future, all at the same time. Perhaps they're five characters in search of an author. Perhaps they're five characters reaching out to each other over an abyss of time and death. Or maybe they're just musical notes. Anyway, "Quintet"—a musical overture.

Equivocate

This scene between the older couple is called "Equivocate." And it was inspired by, well, when my wife got a bad medical report. Her medical reports for a while had been quite good, and then she got a bad one. And we went to a pharmacy in Santa Barbara to get some medicine. And she said, "I think my goose is cooked." But this is not an autobiographical documentary. It's just, as with any artist, taking reality and making it into something. In this case, I wrote a play about time and the mystery of time. Maybe.

Or maybe, it's a play about my mother. Or something else. Who knows? We often don't know what we have created until perhaps years later and sometimes never. I remember an interesting story about a production of *Endgame* I did over thirty years ago. It was a great success and as usual I would come every night and I would watch the performance and give notes to the actors afterwards. Finally, we came to the end of a nice long run. We came to our last performance. The audience was made up mostly of people who had already seen the production many, many times. And so, this being a special occasion, I wanted this last performance to be a special one for them. As the performance progressed, I was appalled. It was one of the worst ever. The actors were terrible. I was so embarrassed, I did something I had never done before. I snuck out of the theater, went to a bar across the street, had a couple of drinks and came back just before the performance ended. Without exception, all of those people, who had seen it many times before, said that that performance was the best ever. You see, I had been able to see it for the first time—truly see it—and I realized what I had done. And faced with that, I was terrified and appalled. I had consciously thought that my production of *Endgame* was about our psychic response to the dangers of thermonuclear war or something along that line. But at that last performance I suddenly understood that it was really about the awful pain of my boyhood relationship to my manic-depressive father. All of which is to say that *Bone Songs* seems at first to be about my first marriage. It's probably about something else, and most of all it's about whatever it seems to you. A friend once pointed out that all the imagery in the play is nature imagery and I grew up in Manhattan. What does that mean?

Waking the Spiders on the Floor:
Things You Should Have Said but Never Could

What we listen to in this scene are the unsaid thoughts, the things the older couple would like to say to each other, and should, but are too terrified. These things start to build up in the marriage, you know, they're things that we're afraid to say because we think we'll hurt the other: "They'll hurt us even more." "They'll kill us." "They'll leave us." These are the thoughts going on inside their heads, which they can't say to each other.

We're Monsters

Couldn't "We're Monsters" be a number out of a musical? This is my fantasy of a confrontation that the older couple might have had. The exhilaration of saying it all. What an incredible relief. Do you remember Bergman's *Cries and Whispers*? The two sisters who had hated each other all their lives finally sit down together and confess their most awful hidden feelings. The moment they do, the hate begins to recede and they begin to experience, for the first time, feelings of love for each other.

Again, it's still in the older couple's heads, and should be read by the actors playing the older couple. But I love to read it myself, and I'm the author, so I can sort of do anything I want.

Arctic Love Song IV: Ah, Youth!

The honeymoon with the young couple starts to get a little rocky. They are all nerves and have a fight. How many of you have gone on a honeymoon? My honeymoon, actually, was a catastrophe. We hadn't even been lovers when we got married. Amazing. I know. But we did become lovers eventually. You know, it was the fifties. And we hardly knew each other. Our first stop was Paris. My parents had given us as a wedding gift, a week in a fancy Parisian hotel. When we came down the first morning for breakfast, there they were in the lobby—my parents had followed us and they had brought along Chiquita's mother! Just as my parents had fled from Stalin and Hitler, we fled from our parents and escaped to London. Somehow or other I had gotten two tickets to *My Fair Lady*, which was a huge hit at the time, and we went. She absolutely hated it. And we had this awful fight. It was the worst fight of our entire marriage—it was so bad. We had tickets to go to Jamaica after London, which in those days by plane took twenty-six hours. We decided that we would go to Jamaica, rest up, and then go back to New York and get a divorce. Thirty-three years later we were still married.

The Hearth of Darkness

I always wanted to direct musicals. Somehow or other I got sidetracked and I ended up as this sort of experimental, avant-garde creature. I don't know what happened. So we now come into the part of the play where things have built up for such a long time with the older couple that they have a fight, a real fight.

Throwing the Bones

Now we're getting to the heart of my darkness. It gets just a little bit darker and then it gets light. This next part is called "Throwing the Bones," and it was directly inspired by my very strange childhood. Whose childhood wasn't strange?

When I was two years old—I almost never saw my parents—I had this German governess and she hated babies who cried. And of course I was crying all the time, because I was lonely and frightened. So she used to put Seconal in my milk. And my mother and grandmother didn't know too much about children, but they did have a suspicious feeling after I had been sleeping for twenty-six hours that something wasn't quite right. So they took me to the doctor and they had to pump my stomach. A sort of family joke for months afterward was that—I can tell people are thinking, Oh my God, who is this person?—I would be crawling around and then just fall down on the floor asleep. I nearly starved to death because my mother and grandmother knew nothing about children and, being Russian, mostly fed me caviar.

I didn't invent any of this—these are my mother's stories, unless, of course, she invented them. Here's another she told: She and my father had gone away on one of their long, mysterious journeys. When they returned to their hotel in Switzerland, my mother couldn't get over the beauty of a tiny baby in a large, English pram at the entrance to the hotel. Finally, the baby's nanny said, "But, madame, he's yours!"

For a long time (even though I've really made peace with my parents, thank God), I used to think of my parents as Macbeth and Lady Macbeth. In fact, my mother's last words (which were said to me) when she was dying in the hospital were: "You know, this whole thing was a mistake. I shouldn't have married him. I shouldn't have had you children. If I get through this alive, I'm going to dump you all and go to Germany. Get me some caviar!" She may have been somewhat crazed at that point, because she hated Germany.

Chiquita's last words couldn't have been more different. While I was downstairs in the hospital, a Catholic priest, uninvited, had entered her room and asked if she wanted last rites. Though a Catholic, she hated the Church for many of the obvious reasons. She refused last rites. When I returned, she asked me if she was dying. I said, "I think so." "I am so blessed," she said, "I have such a beautiful family."

Ruth Nelson, that extraordinary actress from the Group Theatre, who played Nanny in our stage version of *Vanya*, her last words were, "Well, here we go!" And then, of course, there were those of Orson Welles's mother, "Promise me, Orson, promise me you will never do a *Love Boat*!"

We've all had different kinds of gurus in life. I actually do have an Indian guru, a wonderful woman. But, my mother was a guru also, because that thing that she said as she was dying was one of the most important lessons I've ever been given in my whole life—I understood that we have to live the life we have while we have it. And to appreciate it. And if we don't like it we should change it. Let's face it, all of us here tonight are in the tiniest percentage of the most privileged people in the world. Life is too precious to squander.

Do you remember that old movie about the plane crash where the parents are killed, and the little boy in Africa is brought up by apes? Well that was kind of me. No one ever really kissed me or hugged me. No one ever touched me.

When I was at college, I fell madly in love with a young woman, who was at Radcliffe. Her father was America's largest casket manufacturer—what a life I've had so far!—and I was just nuts about her. We'd go to pallbearer conventions together. But I couldn't imagine that this brilliant, beautiful woman could ever love me. We went out for months. We had breakfast, lunch and dinner together, we went to classes together. But I never even dared to touch her hand. She probably thought I was gay. And one night, in Marblehead, Massachusetts, we went out to this very beautiful graveyard and there was a full moon. And she suddenly just decided to go for it, and she grabbed me and kissed me—and I fainted! Having never even been hugged, it was just too much for me. A million volts of erotic electricity surging through my body. Needless to say, the romance flourished. What woman wouldn't have fallen in love with a man who fainted when she kissed him?

How many of you saw *The Shining*? Well *The Shining* was really sort of a documentary about my childhood. I once met Stanley Kubrick and I said to him, "Mr. Kubrick, thank you so much for *The Shining*, it was a documentary about my childhood." And he said, "No, dear boy, it was a documentary about mine."

My dad couldn't stand the fact that I was in the theater. And we used to have these terrible, terrible fights. And when he was about eighty-four, my wife went over to visit him and he said, "I don't understand what's wrong with André, why does he always have to fight with me?" And my wife, Chiquita, said, "You know, I think he thinks you don't respect him." And he said, "Don't respect him? Don't respect him? Of course I respect him. He could have been a great lawyer."

The reason "Throwing the Bones" is in the play is because it shows how some of us, who have been hurt, frightened or ignored in childhood, are afraid of loving, afraid of touching, afraid of reaching out. It's also about the unconscious initiation through childhood trauma of a young shaman—that's yours truly, the Pied Piper of Perry Street.

This story is told as the icebreaker goes into the most terrifying part of Antarctica—the Weddell Sea, which is at the bottom of the world, the worst storms, waves hundreds of feet high. As the characters try to sleep or get through the night, this is the story they hear.

The March of Time

The next little scene is called "The March of Time." Do any of you remember "The March of Time"? You know, the newsreel from the 1940s—"ba ba ba bump ba bum!" You're all too young to remember. And, in a way, it's one of those scenes that they have in musicals. It's just like a little prelude to a song, you know, where somebody says, "Where do you think the play's going to open?" "I don't know, I never thought about that." "Well, maybe we should open it soon." "Yeah, maybe we should." (Launches into song) "We open in Venice! We next play Cremona . . ." (Stops singing) It's that kind of scene. And as a director, I never have music in my plays. And I guess I never have sets. Or costumes. Or even a theater. But this allows us to have a little music cue. —Music, please!

Sex Is a Little Death

At this point, after the fights, the confrontations, the frustration, the nightmares, the storm-tossed waters, a calm begins to settle over their world, over the ocean, over their lives. And slowly love, like a little blossom, begins to break through. The ice begins to melt.

Now we often hear that after a great fight, you can have great sex. So we have a sex scene in this play. Don't tell any of your fundamentalist or neo-con friends! You know, I once got a wonderful idea for a sequel to *My Dinner with André*. I thought, If I lived to be eighty and Wally lived to be seventy, God willing, it would be wonderful if we were in rocking chairs on the porch of some old hotel in the Adirondacks, and all we talked about was the one thing we never talked about in *My Dinner with André*—sex. But we'll never do a sequel without Louis Malle.

⊶≡◎ ◎≡⊷

I let them do all the work and then I can have the orgasm. Going on seventy-one and still going strong. Thank God.

THE ENDINGS

Now we're coming slowly toward the end of the play. And there are actually seven endings. But we're only going to do four tonight. I guess there are so many endings, because I hate endings. And I don't know how to write an ending because I'm not really a playwright. And I hated my wife's ending. And in a way my childhood ended far too early. It ended when I was five years old. You see, my father had this great nose for danger. He left the Soviet Union a year before Stalin came to power. He left Berlin the day Hitler came to power. So when I was five, he got us all out of France just three weeks before the Nazis invaded Poland. And we went to London—got one of the last boats out of France. A blind man helped us with our luggage. As little kids in London, we were outfitted for gas masks. About two months before the German bombing of London began, we crossed the Atlantic. There were two sister ships about a mile apart from each other, and our sister ship was torpedoed. As a little boy, I remember seeing people drowning. We picked up survivors who slept in the corridors of our boat. At last we were safe. In America. In Scarsdale. Isn't that something? Moscow, Berlin, Paris, London and Scarsdale. When my father was in his eighties—he was a Nixon Republican who hated my going on Vietnam peace marches—

126

he, the Great Escape Artist, told me that if he were young again, he would get out of America. Why? He said that both parties are so corrupt, it can only lead to fascism. So, anyway, that day at the age of five, was the end of my childhood. As I said, I hate endings. In fact, I hate endings so much that every time I make a trip I call every friend I have to say good-bye.

The first of the endings is called "As Time Goes By." The scene isn't actually in the play anymore, but I thought it would be fun to read it because of the movie and everything. I also might not be in the theater if we had not lived in Hollywood in the forties. My parents had met Marlene Dietrich in Berlin before Hitler, so that when my dad came to Los Angeles on business, my parents were introduced by her into the movie colony. In fact, I was very heavy, I weighed over two hundred and forty pounds, and Marlene Dietrich (whose daughter was very heavy) helped me solve my weight problem. All kinds of people came to the house—Burns and Allen, Charles Boyer, Basil Rathbone, Lana Turner, Abbott and Costello, Ronald Colman, Jean Renoir—it was amazing. In fact, my mother had two love affairs that I know of, one was with Errol Flynn and the other might have been with Bugsy Siegel. I kid you not. It's true—she was going over to his house the morning his head was blown off. I've had an amazing life. On our tennis court once, I actually saw Garbo and Dietrich on one side of the net and Errol Flynn and Thomas Mann on the other.

(Larry Pine:) "Who taught you to swim?"

Oh yes, Johnny Weissmuller taught me to swim. And I'm a great swimmer.

The first of our endings is called "As Time Goes By."

As Time Goes By

OLDER HE: Play it again, Sam.

OLDER SHE: Are those the cannons or is that the beating of my heart?

OLDER HE: Both, my delicate sweet, the cannons and the beating of your heart. Paris, our city of lights, our boulevard of dreams. The Germans will get here tomorrow, after tomorrow at the latest.

OLDER SHE: Where's Rick? He was going to meet us at five.

OLDER HE: Casablanca. He knew when to get out. Teeny martini?

OLDER SHE: Teeny martini.

OLDER HE: To love.

OLDER SHE: To romance.

OLDER HE: To Fred and Ginger. Nick and Nora. And mostly, my evergreen, to you. What will you do?

OLDER SHE: London, if the Channel boat is still running. Then a Red Cross uniform, roses, champagne, and a bitterly fought victorious war. Pour me another. What about you?

OLDER HE: Oh, I don't know. The Orient Express to Moscow I suppose. Peking on foot. And if I can, Pearl Harbor, the Royal Marines. I'll miss you.

OLDER SHE: I'll miss you, too. Nowhere, not in the deepest crannies of the moon, in the shadows of the Taj Mahal, not on the beaches of Bali, nowhere, will I ever find a man who makes a martini the way you do.

OLDER HE: To martinis, gently stirred and very, very dry.

OLDER SHE: Take care of yourself. Promise?

OLDER HE: I do. If we get through this, after the war, Jerusalem at Eastertime?

OLDER SHE: Jerusalem at Eastertime. You have my promise.

OLDER HE: See ya.

OLDER SHE: See ya, kid.

I was listening to that just now, and I thought, What kind of work do these characters do? They must be independently wealthy.

Iowa

"Iowa" is the most difficult farewell in the play. When my wife got quite ill (she was in a hospital in L.A., thank God not in pain, she had no pain through the whole illness), they put her on some kind of drug. When I got back to my hotel (I had been with her all day), I suddenly thought, There are so many things we've never said to each other, so many things I need to say to her. You know? She kept falling asleep, and I kept saying, "Wake up, honey, there's something I want to say."

This scene is called "Iowa," because some years after she passed away I went to give a workshop at the Iowa Writers Lab. I was given the name of a woman there who was teaching at the Lab, and she was very, very bright. And really quite lovely. And I was staying at this awful motel. It was a dreary, dreary motel, right out of *Psycho*. And I hated going back to that motel. And when we had dinner, I just kept talking about how awful this motel was. She said, quite kindly, "Why don't you come and spend the night with me?" And for some inexplicable reason, I didn't. I went back to my horrible motel room. I got up suddenly at about five o'clock in the morning and I went over to some deserted dining hall. And I found a pencil and paper, and with tears streaming down my cheeks I wrote "Iowa."

So "Iowa" is a death scene. Or sort of. I just don't know about this death thing. One rabbi I studied with saw death as an obscenity. No afterlife. Nothing. Death was basically wrong. An orthodox rabbi. Then there was a kabbalist, an ecstatic, who saw death as the beginning of light. I think about it a lot, you have to at my age. I am a bit like Prospero who says at the end of *The Tempest*, "Every third thought shall be my grave." I did have one quite odd experience though which makes me wonder if death may not be the horrific event we fear it might be. At one point, it was clear that my wife had little time left. She was on very strong drugs, she was hospitalized in California, and we wanted to fly her back to New York so that she could be surrounded by family and friends. We hired a tiny hospital jet to bring her home. On the plane were my daughter, myself, our dog, Topper, and a nurse to watch over my wife. The tiny plane had to land half a dozen times to refuel on small airstrips in the middle of nowhere. My daughter and I would take little walks together each time the plane landed. It should have been the saddest journey imaginable but for some strange, inexplicable reason, each of us found it to be amazingly joyful. There seemed to be some otherworldly sweetness surrounding and protecting us all. So, who knows, the ecstatic kabbalist may be right: Death may be the beginning of light. I do know this though. Since I loathe the Bush Republicans and have contempt for the pusillanimous Democrats, I am thinking of creating a third party whose campaign slogan would be: NO ILLNESS OR DEATH FOR YOU, YOURS OR YOUR PETS. Isn't that a winner? I'll see you all in the Oval Office. We will have even more fun than Clinton did.

So we come to "Iowa." It could be a conventional death scene—she's beginning her last journey, he wants to keep her with him. *Or* perhaps they are each finally able to express their love for each other but it's too late; she's in that strange world between living and dying so neither can really hear each other for most of the scene. *Or* we would be hearing two sides of one person wrestling with a spiritual conflict—"I am so tired, I need to sleep . . ." / "WAKE UP, DON'T GO TO SLEEP!"

One More Turn Around the Garden: Lamb Stew

Remember those wonderful movies in the forties like *The Bishop's Wife* with Loretta Young and Cary Grant? He's not really alive, he's a ghost and she falls in love with him? Well, "One More Turn Around the Garden" was inspired by films like that.

The Explorer has come through the process of the play, from the beginning on the ice when he was grieving and keening, to how he now feels by its end. He says: "It's time," an acceptance, a willingness to let the past go, to let the pain go, to jump into life yet again. Even at his age. After last night's performance, a friend gave me this quote. It's from Aeschylus: "And even in our sleep, pain that could not forget falls drop by drop, upon the heart, and in our despair, against our will, comes wisdom all by the awful grace of God."

Arctic Love Song V: Shackleton's Final Diary Entry

Finally, a beautiful peace settles over the play, just as a beautiful peace has settled over my life. I often feel as if I am a sort of Scrooge or a Job, who finally has found his way home. All the pain and confusion have resulted in some small illumination and an enormous sense of thanksgiving. I am able to do this performance tonight for all of you who have been so responsive and welcoming. I have remarried a wonderful, joyful woman, Cindy, who's a terrific documentary filmmaker. An ecstatic filled with light. She's changed the way I work. She's changed the way I live. She's shown me the world as a place of wonder. I am learning to paint. Do you know Henry Miller's last book, *To Paint Is to Love Again*? I am as passionate about painting as I was when I first worked in the theater so many years ago. We live part of the year on Cape Cod where the light is a mixture between the light in Greece and the light in Brittany where I played as a child. It's beautiful to be out there. Painting. I call my paintings my grandchildren. And sometimes in the middle of the night we'll go out to the studio to see if they are peacefully asleep. We have two pussycats who are like grandchildren. Well, this summer my daughter, Marina, is getting married so I might have a grandchild for real.

And I am very grateful to my children: Marina and my son, Nick (they're both artists), because they have been very tough teachers. They have forced me to be a better human being. More honest. More direct. I am grateful to my parents. They did the best they could. They got me out of Germany and here I am. Alive. I am grateful for my life. I am grateful for my work. And I am extremely grateful to have you here with us tonight helping me develop this play.

Ladies and gentlemen: To absent friends. *(A moment of silence)*

These are the very last four lines of the play. They're wonderful, the last entries in Shackleton's diaries. —MUSIC!!

Production History

André Gregory began writing *Bone Songs* in 1982. As the work progressed, he read the play to an audience of two or three in his living room. It received its first professional production in 1982 at Music-Theatre Group (Lyn Austin, Producer), in Lenox, Massachusetts, in a production directed by Larry Pine.

In 1983, *Bone Songs* was produced by Music-Theatre Group (Lyn Austin, Producer), in New York City, in a production directed by Twyla Tharp and co-directed by André Gregory, with music by the Penguin Cafe Orchestra.

In 1995, Liz Sherman and Scott Cohen produced *Bone Songs* with the Telluride Repertory Theatre Company for the Telluride Theatre Festival at the Sheridan Opera House in Telluride, Colorado. It was directed by Liz Sherman. Scott Cohen was the set designer, Kathy Wahlstrand was the costume designer, James Moody was the light designer, Peter Chadman was the sound designer and Michelle Dahl was the stage manager. The cast included:

YOUNGER SHE	Heather Van Vleet
YOUNGER HE	Jeb Berrier
OLDER SHE	Barbara Betts
OLDER HE	Gerald Martin

In 1996, Liz Sherman, Scott Cohen and André Gregory produced a musical reading of *Bone Songs* at Dartmouth College in Hanover, New Hampshire, sponsored in part by New York Theatre Workshop's annual residency at Dartmouth. It was directed by Liz Sherman, with music by the Alloy Orchestra (Caleb Sampson, Terry Donahue and Ken Winokur). Shawn-Marie Garrett was the dramaturg.

In 2002, Liz Sherman directed a workshop production of *Bone Songs* in New York City. Shawn-Marie Garrett was the dramaturg and Sharon Ott was the stage manager. The cast included:

THE ANCIENT/THE EXPLORER	André Gregory
YOUNGER SHE	Heather Goldenhersh
YOUNGER HE	Neal Huff
OLDER SHE	Dianne Wiest
OLDER HE	Sam Waterston

In 2004, Liz Sherman directed a workshop production of *Bone Songs* in New York City. Shawn-Marie Garrett was the dramaturg and James O'Toole was the stage manager. The cast included:

THE EXPLORER/THE ANCIENT	André Gregory
YOUNGER SHE	Marin Ireland
YOUNGER HE	Jeff Biehl
OLDER SHE	Roberta Maxwell
OLDER HE	Larry Pine

In 2004, *Bone Songs* received a production at Dickinson College in Carlisle, Pennsylvania. Karen Lordi was the director, Margaret McKowen was the costume and lighting designer, Robert Pound was the music director and Norah Turnham was the stage manager. Colin McKeen assisted with lights, Scott McPheeters assisted with movement and Nicole Frachiseur assisted with costumes. The cast included:

THE EXPLORER	James Hallett
YOUNGER SHE	Katy Downing
YOUNGER HE	Jeff Biehl
OLDER SHE	Pamela Gray
OLDER HE	Rob Campbell

In 2005, Liz Sherman directed a workshop production of *Bone Songs* in New York City. Michael Counts was the designer and Jill Jaffe was the composer. The cast included:

THE EXPLORER/YOUNGER HE/OLDER HE	Michael Preston
YOUNGER SHE/OLDER SHE	Polly Styron

In March 2005, *Bone Songs* was performed in Los Angeles at CalArts's REDCAT (Mark Murphy, Executive Director), in a production directed by André Gregory and co-directed by Larry Pine and John Ferraro. The cast included:

THE EXPLORER	André Gregory
YOUNGER SHE/OLDER SHE	Julie Hagerty/Leslie Silva
YOUNGER HE/OLDER HE	Larry Pine

In May 2006, *Bone Songs* was performed at the 92nd Street Y in New York City, in a production directed by André Gregory, with sound by Bruce Odland. The cast included:

THE EXPLORER/THE ANCIENT	André Gregory
YOUNGER SHE/OLDER SHE	Deborah Eisenberg
YOUNGER HE/OLDER HE	Larry Pine

Director, actor, teacher and filmmaker, ANDRÉ GREGORY studied with Sanford Meisner and Martha Graham at the Neighborhood Playhouse, and with Lee Strasberg and Jerzy Grotowski. In 1958, he spent fourteen months as an observer at Brecht's Berliner Ensemble, where he watched the creation of Brecht's *The Resistible Rise of Arturo Ui*, as well as productions of the masterpieces *Mother Courage and Her Children*, *Galileo*, *The Days of the Commune* and *The Threepenny Opera* many, many times.

He produced the American premiere of Jean Genet's *The Blacks*, which ran for five years in New York at the St. Mark's Playhouse. Included in the original cast were James Earl Jones, Roscoe Lee Browne, Cicely Tyson, Louis Gossett, Jr., and Maya Angelou. Many of the finest African American actors of that generation appeared in the production at one time or another, and some went on to create the legendary Negro Ensemble Company.

Gregory was a pioneer of the regional theater movement. He worked as Co-Artistic Director with Stuart Vaughan of the Seattle Repertory Theatre, and as Artistic Director of both the L.A. Inner City Cultural Center (created in Watts just after the Watts riots) and Philadelphia's Theatre of Living Arts. In these theaters, he directed works by Max Frisch, Chekhov, Brecht, Molière, Beckett and others. An enfant terrible to some, he was fired from all three theaters by the boards of directors. Fed up with boards of directors and the regional theater structure, and influenced by Grotowski's *Towards a Poor Theatre* and E. F. Schumacher's *Small Is Beautiful*, in 1968 he created the Manhattan Project with the first graduates of NYU's School of the Arts. Their first production, *Alice in Wonderland*, became one of the hallmark productions of the 1970s, and is recorded in a book that he and Richard Avedon created about the process of turning Lewis Carroll's books into a play. During these Manhattan Project years, he also directed the New York premiere of Wallace Shawn's first play in New York, *Our Late Night*. Since 1970, he's always taken at least one-and-a-half years, and even more, to rehearse a play. During the Manhattan Project's ten years, he taught workshops all over the United States, Canada, Europe, the Mideast and India.

In 1977, Gregory took a twelve-year hiatus from directing. He likes to sometimes equate this hiatus to Eleanora Duse's twelve years away from the theater. During this time, he co-authored and co-starred in, with his now life-long collaborator, Wallace Shawn, the film *My Dinner with André*. This also began a great partnership with Louis Malle, which years later, led to the film *Vanya on 42nd Street*, based on his open rehearsals of *Uncle Vanya*, which were presented in the ruins of the Victory Theatre for small, invited audiences. He and Shawn are now collaborating on a film version of Ibsen's *The Master Builder*, which Shawn has translated, and in which Shawn plays the Master Builder. In 2000, he directed Shawn's *The Designated Mourner*, which was presented in the ruins of a defunct men's club on Wall Street. It featured Shawn, Deborah Eisenberg and Larry Pine. Gregory's production of Beckett's *Endgame*, which was performed in 2005 in an unfinished Donald Judd building in the Marfa, Texas, desert, under the auspices of the Chinati Foundation, will be made into a documentary in spring 2007.

Other than Shawn, long-time collaborators with whom he's worked for more than thiry years include Larry Pine, Gerry Bamman and Eugene Lee.

As an actor, he's appeared in a dozen Hollywood films, most notably *The Last Temptation of Christ*, directed by Martin Scorsese, in which he played John the Baptist.

Gregory has two children by his first marriage, Nick and Marina, both artists. His most recent passions are his wife, Cindy, and oil painting.